TOLERANCE

Learning to accept people of different cultures helps to foster tolerance.

THE VALUES LIBRARY

TOLERANCE

Kevin Osborn

THE ROSEN PUBLISHING GROUP, INC.
NEW YORK

Published in 1990, 1993 by The Rosen Publishing Group, Inc.
29 East 21st Street, New York NY 10010

Revised Edition, 1993

Printed in the United States of America

Library of Congress Cataloging-in Publication Data

Osborne, Kevin, 1958-
Tolerance / Kevin Osborne
(The Values library)
Includes bibliographical references and index.
Summary: Examines the meaning of tolerance, its importance in modern society; and
the kinds of intolerance or prejudice that may prevent people from respecting differences
in others.
   ISBN 0-8239-1508-5
   1. Tolerance—Juvenile literature. 2. Prejudices—Juvenile literature. 3. Interpersonal
relations—Juvenile literature. [1. Toleration. 2. Prejudices.] I. Title. II. Series.
BJ1431.059   1990
179'.8—dc20   90-35404
                                                              CIP
                                                              AC

C O N T E N T S

INTRODUCTION

THE MEANING OF TOLERANCE

TOLERANCE IS IMPORTANT FOR EVERYONE. It is needed in almost every situation where people live or work together. Whether we talk about peace between nations or harmony between friends, tolerance plays a role.

The key to tolerance is accepting people as they are. Being tolerant of others means allowing them to be different from you. One way to accept others is to learn about them. Most intolerant people know very little about the people they dislike. The most common cause of intolerance is *ignorance*. Ignorance means not knowing the whole truth about someone. With little knowledge of others, an intolerant person will make *assumptions* about others. Assumptions are guesses. Assumptions are very often false. Assumptions can be made because of *prejudices*. Prejudices are unfair assumptions about others. Usually, prejudices are based on race, religion, sex, or age.

How does a person avoid making unfair assumptions about others? One important step is to keep an open mind.

Another important step is to learn about people who are different from you. The more you learn about others, the less you will have to guess. When you have the facts, you will not make as many unfair assumptions in life. *Honest communication* with others is also important for tolerance. So is the ability to *compromise* (give and take). We will talk more about these qualities in the chapters that follow.

In this book, we will see how tolerance plays an important role in all our lives. We will see tolerance and intolerance at work in world politics. We will discuss tolerance throughout our history. We will see how the United States and Canada were founded on the idea of tolerance. And we will talk about tolerance in our daily lives. We will see how important understanding and acceptance are in our families, in our schools, and in our communities.

Almost everyone can benefit from being more tolerant. Tolerance is not always easy. Many times, learning to be tolerant can feel like work. It can mean admitting you were wrong or unfair. Sometimes it means looking at a person or situation over and over again. And other times tolerance means taking a chance and trusting someone else. But tolerance is well worth the effort. If you become tolerant you will become more kind and fair to the world around you. And that will truly make you a better person.

Sometimes people make quick judgments about others and exclude them from their group,

INTOLERANCE IN OUR WORLD

EXAMPLES OF INTOLERANCE ARE EVERYWHERE IN OUR WORLD. In
the United States, for example, many people are disliked
simply because of their race. African Americans, Chinese,
Koreans, and Native Americans are just a few groups who
often suffer from the hatred and prejudices of others.

Many people in America are disliked because of their
religion. Anti-Semitism, which is hatred of Jews, is not
uncommon in America. Jews have been shunned by many
different societies throughout the ages. Intolerance is
something they have battled against for thousands of years.

Still other people in America suffer because of their
sexual choices. Homosexuals (people who prefer to have
sex with members of their same gender) often suffer
intolerance from others. In many cases, homosexuals are
insulted, threatened, and even harmed by individuals who
cannot tolerate the private lives of others.

But America is not the only place in the world where intolerance exists. For many years, South Africa was ruled by *apartheid*. This meant that there were laws that separated blacks and whites throughout the society. Blacks were educated in inferior schools and had to live in poor

Until 1865, African
Americans were bought
and sold as slaves.

---

neighborhoods. They were subject to different laws than whites. Recently this practice has begun to change.

In Germany, there has been an increase in hate crimes and hate groups. These groups want to get many "non-German" groups out of Germany. In the early 1990s, there were many cases of people being beaten and attacked by members of these hate groups.

There is probably no country on Earth that does not have intolerant people. And it is probably impossible to get rid of all intolerance in the future. Intolerance is not new. It has existed for as long as human beings have lived.

Ideas Based on Tolerance

Tolerance is one of the most important foundations in a democracy. That is because democracy only works when everyone has a chance to voice their opinions. When people from different cultures can be equally protected and cared for by their government, they enjoy the best that democracy has to offer.

In a democracy, the *majority* rules. That means the opinions shared by the most people often have the most power. But the majority is not always right. In many cases, tolerance and fairness have demanded that laws be made to go against the majority's wishes. Before 1920,

Women won the right to
vote in 1920.

women did not have the right to vote. Men, who were the
majority in Congress, refused women that basic right. The
women's *suffrage movement* (voting movement) finally
convinced male lawmakers that the law had to be
changed. Another example of majority injustice was slavery. Before 1865, slavery was legal in America. The
majority ruled that this was the law of the land. But op-
posing voices persuaded many people that slavery was
wrong. The Civil War settled the slavery issue in America.
When the South lost the war, slavery officially lost with it.
Even today, there are still many laws that are unfair to
certain citizens. Lawmakers and voters must be tolerant of
the wishes and rights of everyone in a democracy. And
they must make sure no group, no matter how small, is
denied their rights to freedom and happiness.

The U.S. Constitution has special rules that protect the
rights of all people, even if they are in the minority. These
rules are called the Bill of Rights.

The Bill of Rights was designed to protect the rights of
people who may not have a strong voice in government.
A majority in a democracy can always say what it pleases.
These amendments (rules) attempted to promise the same
freedoms to the minority. The Bill of Rights promises that
intolerance will not be allowed to silence the minority. Its
writers knew that democracy works only when all the
people have a chance to speak out.

Nations, like people, can only grow through change. But people never change unless they start to see things in a new way. The writers of the Constitution knew that America needed laws to make sure people's personal intolerances did not deny rights to others. These laws forced people to provide basic freedoms to everyone. They forced them to listen to the minority. Remaining open to minority opinions allows the majority to see things differently. Tolerance permits people to change and grow.

What Tolerance Means to a Minority Group

Minority groups need to practice tolerance, too. Members of minority groups often need to fight hard to win their rights. In this struggle for freedoms, tempers can flare. Minorities sometimes give in to a widespread prejudice against the majority.

The Problem in Ireland

Northern Ireland, for instance, today has a Protestant majority and Catholic minority. Four hundred years ago, the people of Northern Ireland were almost all Catholic. But in the early seventeenth century (1600s), England's King James I wanted to change that. He sent thousands of Protestants from Scotland and England to settle in Ireland. Protestants soon became the majority in Northern Ireland.

But many Irish Catholics have thought of Protestants as invaders ever since.

Some Catholics today still view almost all Protestants as their enemies. But seeing all Protestants as evil and mean spirited is unfair. Both the minority and the majority are made up of individual people. Some are good and some are bad. Some are mean and some are nice. Members of minority groups need to remember this fact.

Minorities do need to stand up for their rights. They should never have to submit to mistreatment from a majority group. But intolerance and violence will never lead to a solution. Violence and prejudice keep people apart. In Northern Ireland, the Catholic minority deserves a political voice. Everyone in Ireland deserves good jobs and adequate housing. But continuing violence on both sides has not won these rights for everyone. Intolerance has only increased conflict and problems.

Without mutual tolerance, the war in Northern Ireland will never end. A peaceful solution might still be found. But the two groups must first learn to treat each other with tolerance. Catholics and Protestants need to join together as a community. They will never find answers to their problems as long as they remain divided in their prejudices. Like any groups in conflict with each other, they need to find common ground. Mutual tolerance provides the only possible path toward peace.

2

THE IMPORTANCE OF TOLERANCE TODAY

TODAY, MORE THAN EVER, TOLERANCE IS IMPORTANT between individuals and nations. People can travel easily across the globe in super-fast jets. Fax machines, computers, cable television, and other satellite communications have also changed our lives. They have meant that people can speak easily to one another from thousands of miles away.

All our technology has probably helped to increase tolerance in our world. In some ways, the world is a much smaller place with this variety of technology. Canadians can watch Russians on their local news programs. Italians can send faxes to China in seconds. Australians can have computer "discussions" with Africans.

How does this create more tolerance in our world? Because the world is smaller, there is likely to be more communication between people of different cultures and backgrounds. This increase in communication brings increased exposure of people to one another. This is a chance to learn more about others. And more knowledge of others means more tolerance of others!

16

Getting along with different kinds of people is an example of tolerance.

Tolerance in the Nuclear Age

Computers and fax machines are relatively harmless. But some of our technology is not. Nuclear weapons, for example, are very dangerous. Since the 1940s, people have known how to make nuclear weapons. Today, these weapons are capable of destroying our planet. There are many people who say that such dangerous technology helps to promote tolerance. These people say that such weapons force nations to compromise with each other. No one wants another nation to use a nuclear weapon. To avoid this, nations are forced to talk to one another. In recent years, talk of reducing nuclear weapons throughout the world has become widespread. In years to come, many of these weapons may be disarmed.

A Great Mix of Cultures

Countries such as Canada, the United States, Israel, Australia, and England are nations of immigrants. Through the years, people from less tolerant countries have come to these nations for a better life.

Many Americans and Canadians take great pride in their countries' mix of people. They say that many different cultures in their countries make their societies rich and interesting. They also say that tolerance is served when people of different backgrounds can live peacefully in the same country together.

Immigrants bring their customs and beliefs to the new communities where they settle.

The United Nations was founded so that all the peoples of the world can meet and discuss problems.

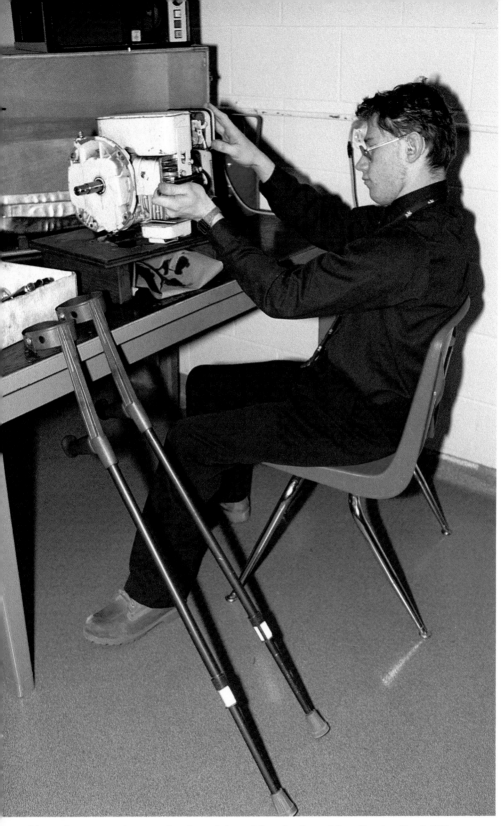

Handicapped people should not be judged by their disabilities.

3

WHAT'S THE DIFFERENCE?

INTOLERANCE USUALLY COMES ABOUT IN RESPONSE to physical differences or differences in beliefs. This has been true all through history.

Difference in Appearance

Physical differences often provide the spark for intolerance. That is probably because they are so easily seen. When we see strangers, we notice physical things at once. In an instant, we know the color of their skin. We can tell whether they are men or women. We can guess their height and weight. And we can see any physical handicap.

Many people assume other things, based on these surface signs alone. They may assume, unfairly, that a person with dark skin is also uneducated and poor. They may guess that because a person is a woman, she is weak and helpless. This kind of guess, based on just one physical feature, is called a *stereotype*. Stereotypes are wrong more often than they are right. And believing in stereotypes shows intolerance.

Imagine seeing a woman in a wheelchair, for example. What else does that really tell you about her? You know that she does not have full use of her legs. And that is all you can really tell. Unfortunately, some people believe a physically disabled person has a mental handicap, too. But most people in wheelchairs are just the same as anyone else. Their only difference is their physical disability. They do not want others to treat them differently. They want the same respect and tolerance that every one of us deserves.

As individuals, we need to learn to tolerate physical differences. People come in many sizes: large and small, skinny and fat, muscular and flabby. People come in many colors: black, white, red, yellow, and brown. And people come in two sexes: male and female. But the fact that a person is a woman tells us only one thing: her sex. And the fact that her skin is quite dark tells us only that she is probably an African American. You have to get to know her to find out what she is really like. And you will need to ignore surface differences if you want to get to know her. This is tolerance in action.

Difference in Beliefs

The other major spark of intolerance is differences in beliefs. *Religious beliefs* tell a person's deepest understanding of the meaning of life. For this reason, religious differences can cause the strongest hatred. Religious intolerance in fact goes against the teachings of most religions. Christianity, Judaism, Islam, and Buddhism all preach the ideals of tolerance and good will. These religions teach that even those with different religious beliefs deserve tolerance and respect. Religions teach that practicing these ideals adds to the peace and unity of humankind.

In spite of these teachings, religious intolerance has produced some of history's most violent wars. The bloody Crusades were wars between Christians and Moslems for the ownership of the Holy Land (Palestine, which is now Israel). The Crusades lasted for two centuries, from 1095 to 1291 A.D. Even today, religious intolerance is the cause of fighting in Northern Ireland and in the Middle East.

Differences in *political beliefs* can also set off intolerance. People often have strong beliefs about the role of government in their lives. The United States, for example, has many political parties. Each party represents a different set of opinions. The Democratic and Republican

Everyone has a right to worship in his or her own way.

parties are the largest and best known. But Americans
can also choose the Communist, Conservative, Liberal,
Libertarian, and Socialist parties, among many others. The
Constitutional right of free speech guarantees all Americans this choice.

In the 1950s, however, political intolerance in the
United States reached a dangerous level. From 1950 to
1954, Wisconsin Senator Joseph McCarthy led the Senate
in a "Communist witch hunt." The Senate investigated
rumored "Communists" in the government, in the Army,
and in the entertainment industry. Anyone who admitted
that they had once belonged to the Communist Party was
called a traitor. Some of these so-called "Communists"
had left the Communist Party twenty or thirty years earlier.
But even they were unfairly stripped of their jobs. In
addition, they were illegally "blacklisted" (barred from any
future employment).

In April and May of 1954, the Senate hearings were
televised into millions of American homes. Senator
McCarthy's intolerance and his viciousness to witnesses
quickly turned public opinion against him. Several
months later, the Senate publicly criticized McCarthy for
his bullying and his attacks. This kind of intolerance has
been condemned in America ever since. Today we know
it as "McCarthyism."

In the 1950s, Senator Joseph McCarthy *(right)* accused many people of being un-American.

Tolerating Differences of Opinion

All of us need to learn how to tolerate differences of opinion and belief. This is just as important as teaching ourselves to look beyond physical differences.

A difference of opinion doesn't have to drive people apart. You may believe that Willie Mays was the best baseball player of all time. Your best friend may say, "No way! It was Babe Ruth!" You might even get into a heated argument about who was right. But your friend is not stupid just because he disagrees with you. You both have a common love for baseball. And this common ground can help you be best friends even while you disagree.

The same thinking applies to religious and political differences. People everywhere believe in many different religions. Some people, called atheists, believe in none of them. But people have many things in common in spite of differences in religious beliefs. Jews, Christians, Muslims, Buddhists, and atheists just believe in different things.

People can be intelligent and patriotic no matter what political beliefs they hold. It does not matter if they are liberal or conservative, Republican or Democrat, or independent. People can go forward toward common goals and beliefs. But they must move beyond religious and political differences. This is tolerance in action.

Everyone Can Teach Us Something

We can all learn a lot from the many different people in the world. But we cannot learn from others if we shut out everyone who seems a little different. Intolerance cuts us off from many chances for change and growth. Tolerance is important not only because it is the "right" way to treat other people. Tolerance also allows us to learn from others. It helps us to grow as people—and to grow closer to one another.

In today's world people of different backgrounds must live and work together.

4

TOLERANCE AND INTOLERANCE IN OUR PAST

HEROES THROUGHOUT HISTORY HAVE DEMONSTRATED the value of tolerance. Very few, however, have received the world's praise for keeping an open mind. Tolerance seldom commands this kind of attention. History and the news media most often report conflict. War, revolution, and acts of violence appear on television. They appear on the front pages of newspapers and in history books. Keeping an open mind helps to *avoid* conflict and maintain peace. But peace and quiet rarely make news. So some of the greatest examples of tolerance in history may have gone unreported.

The peaceful settlement of any dispute calls for both sides to look beyond their differences. Opponents need to see what ideas they share. But to do this they need to treat each other with tolerance. Tolerance is the key to settling conflicts and making peace. In settings of war or violent prejudice, speaking out for tolerance becomes an

Strife between Christians and Muslims in Lebanon has resulted in many years of war and violence.

act of heroism. In times of war, heroes who attempt to make peace stand out in sharp contrast. The heroes who call for mutual tolerance are the world's peacemakers.

Intolerance in Nazi Germany

The twentieth century offers many examples of intolerance. One of the worst examples was Nazi Germany during the 1930s and 1940s. The Nazis, led by Adolf Hitler, tried to destroy all minority races in Germany. Hitler hated the minority races. He believed that Aryans (white Germanic or Nordic peoples) were a superior "master race." He saw all others as members of "inferior" races. During Hitler's twelve years of power, the Nazis murdered *millions* of Europe's minority citizens, especially Jews.

Hitler took power in Germany in 1933. That year, Germany opened its first concentration camps at Dachau, Oranienburg, and Buchenwald. At first these camps were like detention centers. "Inferior" people were "concentrated" away from members of the "master race." Many of these centers were work camps, in the beginning. Things for which these camps became infamous did not happen right away. Some of the people sent to the camps were Jews. Others were gypsies, homosexuals and some Catholics. People who opposed the Nazis were also sent to the camps.

One of the worst episodes of Nazi intolerance happened on November 9-10, 1938. In a single night, Nazis
burned down 267 synagogues all over Germany. Almost
30,000 Jews were arrested. This night became known as
Kristallnacht, or "The Night of Broken Glass." The shop
windows of all Jewish owned stores and windows in the
synagogues were smashed. It is still remembered today
as one of the world's ugliest nightmares.

During World War II, the Germans overran most of
Europe. The Jews in Europe were herded into death
camps. Imprisoned Jews, political prisoners, homosexuals,
and gypsies were treated as slave labor. Many became
the subjects of horrible medical experiments. Millions
died. In all, the Nazis murdered more than ten million
people. And millions more were imprisoned, enslaved,
and tortured between 1933 and 1945.

Heroes of Tolerance

Against this horrifying background, thousands of
heroes stood up to oppose the Nazis. Many non-Jews
fought against the Nazis by hiding Jewish children in their
homes. These brave families sheltered Jewish children
and reared them as their own. In Denmark, France,
Holland and several other nations conquered by the Nazis,
unnamed heroes hid Jews in their homes. These heroes
risked their own lives to protect the lives of others. They

often created false passports and official papers. These helped Jews to disguise themselves and escape. Many people helped Jews escape to Sweden, Switzerland, and Spain. Those countries were "neutral." They had agreements not to fight with Germany. Jews were safer there.

One of the greatest heroes of this time was Raoul Wallenberg. Wallenberg sheltered thousands of Hungarian Jews in "protected houses." He protected the houses by flying the flags of Sweden and other neutral countries from their roofs. The Nazis could not attack these shelters without declaring war on these nations. Wallenberg shielded as many as 35,000 Jews and others in this way.

Wallenberg also brought food and clothing to Jewish prisoners. His efforts to fight against the Germans made Wallenberg a target. Several times they threatened him, to try to make him stop. But he continued, despite the threats. Wallenberg could not close his eyes to injustice.

From the Nazi abuse and murder of Jews and others we can learn important lessons about tolerance. The most important lesson is that *tolerance requires action.* Tolerance does not mean simply *allowing* others to be different. It means taking action to protect people's right to be different. Especially during times of intolerance, prejudice can explode into violence and murder.

Tolerance is more than overcoming our own prejudice. It means actively working to overcome the prejudice of others. Intolerance of any kind—racial, sexual, religious, or political—is a threat to individual rights.

The United States Civil Rights Movement

Heroes who stood up for tolerance have fought in the United States, too. In the 1950s and 1960s, these heroes led the fight for civil rights for African Americans. The Reverend Dr. Martin Luther King, Jr. and Supreme Court Justice Thurgood Marshall struggled for many years to gain justice. Their efforts have won support for civil rights from white Americans and African Americans alike. These two groups united for civil rights for all Americans. They have worked together to continue the fight against intolerance and injustice.

Victories for Tolerance

Thurgood Marshall won the first real victory against American racial intolerance. In 1954 he was a lawyer for the National Association for the Advance of Colored People (NAACP). Marshall argued against racial segregation in the famous Supreme Court case of *Brown vs. Board of Education of Topeka, Kansas.* His arguments convinced all nine justices on the Supreme Court. They ruled by a vote of 9-0 that racial segregation in public schools was illegal. This decision was a great victory for racial tolerance. For the first time, the government stated

Martin Luther King, Jr., was an important leader in the civil rights struggle of the 1960s.

that all Americans—African American, whites, and others—deserved the same quality education.

A Victory in the Streets for Tolerance

Even after Thurgood Marshall's victory, other rights were still denied to African Americans. The Reverend Dr. Martin Luther King, Jr., led a non-violent protest movement aimed at winning those rights. King called for peace, unity, and justice between African Americans and whites. His call for peace contrasted sharply with the intolerance of some whites who opposed him. The sheriff of Birmingham, Alabama, for example, Eugene "Bull" Connor, ordered police to attack King and other peaceful protesters. Police turned high-pressure fire hoses and trained police dogs on the demonstrators. Most Americans were shocked to see this violence on their television screens. The public soon joined in support of Dr. King's movement.

In August 1963, King led 250,000 Americans in a March on Washington, D.C. Americans of every color came together from all over the country. They gathered on the steps of the Lincoln Memorial. There King delivered one of the most stirring speeches in American history. "I have a dream," he exclaimed, "that my four little children will one day live in a nation where they will not be judged by the color of their skin, but by the content of their character." Dr. King's efforts to promote tolerance and justice earned him the 1964 Nobel Peace Prize.

Intolerance in the 1990s

Thurgood Marshall and Dr. Martin Luther King, Jr. made great efforts to bring tolerance to the world. Much of their work has made the United States a better place in which to live. But the civil rights movement did not end the prejudice and hatred towards blacks in America. And it did not end intolerance between Americans of different religions, races, or sexes.

Thurgood Marshall was a civil rights lawyer who argued in front of the United States Supreme Court. He was later appointed to the court as one of the nine justices.

Today, in America, intolerance often lies beneath the surface of daily life. In many large cities, intolerance does not go away when people live near each other. In some cases, it can be held back enough to allow people to exist side by side. But intolerance can not be hidden for very long. Sooner or later, it will explode. It is sad, but the poverty and pressures of city life often make it hard for people to appreciate those who are different from themselves.

A Campaign of Intolerance in Louisiana

In November 1991, a man named David Duke ran a political campaign in Louisiana that was based on intolerance. Duke was a former head of the Ku Klux Klan and a longtime member of the Nazi party. He had spent much of his life preaching hatred to others.

During his campaign, Duke appealed to voters with his ideas about the need for racial purity in America. He said that Jews and blacks, in particular, were causing America's biggest problems. The people of Louisiana had suffered a bad economy for many years. Many citizens were out of work, a great deal were homeless. They were eager to blame their problems on other people. David Duke gave those angry citizens a voice. But Duke was also giving a voice to intolerance. He was telling people that it was okay to hate and to blame others.

In many parts of the United States, before civil rights laws were passed, African Americans were not allowed to mix with whites.

On November 16, 1991, Louisiana voters went to the polls. David Duke came very close to winning his race for the office of governor of Louisiana. By the time all the votes were counted, however, David Duke had lost his campaign. But he won in many other ways. He made a strong showing in the race. That told him he had much support. People all across America saw him on television and in the newspapers. His message was sent across the land. Duke later said that he would use that exposure to run for president in 1992, but he never did.

A New Tolerance in Eastern Europe and Soviet Society

We have already read about intolerance based on race, religion, and sex. In many democratic countries, these are the most common forms of intolerance. But *political intolerance* has also been a major problem throughout the world. Political intolerance means people are punished if they do not agree with their ruling government.

For many decades, the people of the old Soviet Union (USSR) and Eastern Europe suffered from political intolerance. These people lived in Communist countries, where free speech and criticism of the government were not allowed. When Joseph Stalin ruled the USSR in the 1930s and 1940s, he ruled with an "iron hand." That meant he controlled the citizens very carefully. And he limited their freedoms. Under Stalin, millions of Soviet citizens were tortured and murdered because they were thought to have critical opinions of their government.

By the late 1980s, many people in the USSR and Eastern Europe were growing more unhappy with communism. Popular democratic movements in Poland (led by Lech Walesa) and other countries soon became powerful forces for change.

The time between 1989 and 1991 in the USSR and Eastern Europe was marked by many amazing events. During those few years, communism was almost completely erased in Czechoslovakia, Hungary, Poland, Romania, Bulgaria, and Yugoslavia. Even the Soviet Union, which had been the center of communism throughout the world, did away with communism by August of 1991. It was during that month that a few Soviet government officials tried to take power away from President Mikhail Gorbachev and Russian President Boris Yeltsin. But their plan backfired. The people of the Soviet Union revolted. And the people's cry was for democracy.

With the movement toward democracy in these countries, tolerance grew. Without the harsh restrictions of communism, citizens began to speak their minds freely. Newspapers were free to print articles about politics. Television programs could show people discussing different opinions. No one was in danger of being arrested for

In 1991, symbols of old Soviet communism—like this giant statue of V.I. Lenin—were taken down throughout the republics of the new commonwealth.

what they believed. The people of these countries had demanded that their government be more tolerant. And the governments saw that they had to respond. By the end of 1991, new governments had taken hold throughout Eastern Europe and the old Soviet republics (many of which became independent states). Eleven of the republics from the USSR declared independence and formed the Commonwealth of Independent States. These great changes were not only a triumph for democracy, they were a triumph for tolerance as well.

You Can Change Intolerance

The work of Martin Luther King and Thurgood Marshall showed us how people can change intolerance and injustice in our society. The people of the old USSR and Eastern Europe demanded tolerance from their leaders. By banding together, they changed entire governments nearly overnight. The people who did not vote for David Duke also changed the world. They did not allow such a man to gain the power he sought. Protesters like Nelson Mandela of South Africa are still struggling to end intolerance of blacks in their country. These examples show us that individuals can have a great effect on tolerance. If people work to erase hatred and prejudice, they can succeed. The first step is keeping your heart and your mind open and having a healthy respect for others.

Gandhi used non-violent protest to help free India from British rule.

5

PEACE THROUGH TOLERANCE

PERHAPS THE GREATEST CHAMPION OF TOLERANCE in modern times is Mohandas Gandhi. Gandhi became the spiritual and political leader of India during the first half of this century. He united the people of India despite their religious differences. And he urged them toward non-violence in all protests.

From 1894 to 1914, Gandhi lived in South Africa. There, he led protests against racial bigotry aimed at the Indian community. Over this twenty-year period he developed an unusual method of non-violent protest. This technique would serve as a model for all peacemakers of the twentieth century. Gandhi urged all Indians to obey three rules of protest.

- Always respect your opponents.
- Always keep an open mind.
- Look for creative ways to solve problems that will be fair and acceptable to all sides in conflict.

All three of these rules demand tolerance.

In 1914, Gandhi returned to his native country. For over thirty years he struggled to unite the people of India. He urged them all to share in the common goal of winning the nation's independence. Gandhi first fought for the rights of the "untouchables," the lowest social class in India. Then he worked to unite Hindus and Muslims in their struggle for independence. In time, India overcame both class and religious differences with mutual tolerance. The united people of India achieved their common goal. They gained their freedom from Great Britain in 1947.

Against Gandhi's opposition, India was split into two separate nations. The two new nations were divided by religion: Hindu India and Muslim Pakistan. Tolerance had helped win India's independence. But this tolerance was not strong enough to keep the nation united after reaching its goal.

Gandhi's life provided a model of tolerance in protest. This model has shown to all those who followed him the way toward non-violent change.

Winners of the Nobel Peace Prize

The greatest peacemakers of this century all learned a great deal from Gandhi's teachings. Dr. Martin Luther King, Jr., used Gandhi's methods of protest in leading the fight for civil rights in the United States. Mairead Corrigan and Betty Williams tried to unite Catholics and Protestants after a long history of conflict in Northern Ireland. Bishop Desmond Tutu has become a voice of protest against the intolerant system of apartheid in South Africa.

Each of these heroes has followed Gandhi's example. Each has chosen to follow a path of peaceful protest instead of violence. Each has promoted tolerance against a background of intolerance or violence. Each of these heroes has won the Nobel Peace Prize. Their commitment to non-violence in their struggle for peace and justice has won them great honor.

Birth of the Peace People

The region now known as Northern Ireland has been torn with conflict since the 1600s. That is when England sent thousands of Protestants to settle the area. Today, the Protestant majority rules the country through its military and economic power. The one million Protestants of Northern Ireland want to hold on to their power. But 500,000 Catholics oppose them. This Catholic minority

Betty Williams *(left)* and Mairead Corrigan founded the Community of Peace People to help bring peace to Northern Ireland.

wants better jobs, better housing, and more political power.

In the end, however, many Catholics want to see Northern Ireland reunited with the rest of Ireland. This would change the Protestant majority into a minority. They would quickly lose all political power. Both sides in this conflict desperately want to win their goals. Sadly, both Catholics and Protestants in this small country have often turned to violence.

In 1976, Betty Williams and Mairead Corrigan decided that this violence would have to stop. On August 10, 1976, a runaway car in Belfast, Northern Ireland, had killed three children and seriously injured their mother. The car's driver, a Catholic militant, had been shot and killed trying to get away from the police. Betty Williams witnessed this tragic automobile crash. Within hours, she began marching from door to door in Belfast, carrying a petition for peace. Williams read the petition on television two nights later. She had already gathered 6,000 signatures calling for peace and tolerance.

Mairead Corrigan, whose niece and nephews had died in the crash, also appeared on television. She appealed for an end to the violence and bloodshed. On August 14, Mairead Corrigan and Betty Williams led 10,000 women in a march for peace through the streets of Belfast. Together,

Corrigan and Williams formed Women for Peace (later
called the Community of Peace People). This organization
united Protestants and Catholics in the cause of peace.
The Peace People organized rallies and marches. They
issued pamphlets. They urged peace and tolerance
among both Catholics and Protestants. They urged *all* of
the people of Northern Ireland to move toward peace and
mutual tolerance.

Corrigan and Williams wanted to increase peaceful
contact between Protestants and Catholics. For this reason, the Peace People founded youth clubs and peace
houses, and sponsored sports activities. These efforts
succeeded in getting Catholics and Protestants involved in
their local communities *together.* Corrigan and Williams
tried to replace a tradition of hatred with a new sense of
tolerance. They were awarded the 1976 Nobel Peace
Prize. The world praised their attempts to bridge religious
and political divisions.

How to Encourage Tolerance

Corrigan and Williams have not succeeded in ending
the conflict in Northern Ireland. But they and the Peace
People have shown a heroic commitment to tolerance.
Their efforts illustrate two important ways of promoting
tolerance.

Increasing Contact Between the Different Groups

Protestants and Catholics had long shunned each other in Northern Ireland. But Corrigan and Williams brought these two groups together. The two groups had their first real chance to discover that they had something in common. Hatred and violence were destroying their homes and their neighborhoods. It was killing their children. Both groups agreed that the violence had to stop.

Bringing the two groups together was an important step. But it was only a beginning. For tolerance to spread, the two groups would have to work together.

Encouraging Cooperation Between the Two Competing Groups

Corrigan and Williams tried to promote tolerance and end prejudice in another way, too. They founded youth clubs and peace associations. Both women wanted to see Protestants and Catholics working together toward common goals. The two groups certainly had political and religious disagreements. But they still shared some common dreams. Both wished for peace and for the promise of their children's future. The two groups would have to cooperate to move toward these dreams. They needed to set aside their differences and work together as one. In other words, they had no choice but to practice tolerance.

Peace in the Middle East

In 1978, the Nobel Committee honored Egyptian President Anwar Sadat and Israeli Prime Minister Menachem Begin. Israel had become a nation in 1948. But Egypt, like other Arab nations, had refused to accept Israel's right to exist. For thirty years, Arab and Israeli neighbors had treated each other with hostility and suspicion. Several times this hatred had erupted into war.

In 1978, however, Sadat and Begin met with U.S. President Jimmy Carter. It was the first time the leaders of these two nations had ever come together. At this historic meeting, they worked out a peace treaty between Egypt

Anwar Sadat *(left)* of
Egypt and Menachem
Begin *(right)* of Israel
signed a peace treaty
with the help of President
Jimmy Carter *(center)* of
the United States.

---

and Israel. The two nations recognized each other's right
to exist despite their differences. This was a truly heroic
demonstration of tolerance. For the first time, these
leaders had decided to work together toward peace.

A Divided People Moving Toward Peace

In 1984, the Nobel Committee recognized another
supporter of tolerance. Bishop Desmond Tutu, a South
African pastor, won the Peace Prize that year. Tutu has
been one of the leading voices against the intolerant system of apartheid. Tutu has preached racial tolerance to
both blacks and whites. At the same time, Tutu urges
action in the pursuit of peace and justice. Tutu believes
that people who do not *protest* against intolerance are
actually supporting it. He insists that people need to
stand up against intolerance and injustice. That is the
only way to move toward justice.

Dr. Martin Luther King, Jr., Mairead Corrigan and Betty
Williams, Anwar Sadat and Menachem Begin, and Bishop
Desmond Tutu have all won the Nobel Peace Prize. The
Nobel Committee has saluted many other heroes of tolerance. Most winners of the Nobel Peace Prize have tried
to unite regions divided by conflict. They have called for
tolerance to bring different people together.

Getting to know someone of a different race can teach you that people are more alike than they are different from one another.

6

OPEN EARS, OPEN EYES, AND AN OPEN MIND

LAURA WILDER HAD NEVER REALLY MET ANY AFRICAN AMERICANS until Barbara Kendall moved to town. Almost everyone who lived in her small town was white. She *had* seen some African Americans while visiting her grandparents in Chicago. But she had never stopped to talk to them. Laura thought that Barbara was beautiful. With her dark skin and deep brown eyes, she looked stunning. But Laura wondered what Barbara was really like. Did that dark skin make Barbara different from Laura herself?

Laura knew how some people in town would answer that question. Some people thought that the color of Barbara's skin made a big difference. She had heard some of the whispering over the summer. When the Kendalls had first moved into town, the talk had started.

Chapter Six

Some of the Wilders' friends had snapped that crime would go up. Others complained that real estate values would go down because 'blacks' were moving into town. She had heard others worrying that their children's education would get worse. "The schools will have to slow down to *their* speed," barked the owner of the hardware store.

But Laura had also heard her parents' angry response to these words. "Nonsense!" they had shouted. "The Kendalls have just as much right to live here as we do."

Still, she wondered what Barbara Kendall was really like. Laura was a little scared, but she decided that she would have to find out for herself.

Laura went up to Barbara before school and introduced herself. "Hi, I'm Laura Wilder. I can show you around school if you need any help." They talked and joked together for the rest of the day. Laura found out that Barbara loved to play the piano—just like she did. And both of them wanted to try out for the basketball team in a few months. By the end of the afternoon, some of Laura's other friends had joined them. And when they got to know Barbara, they liked her very much. Within a couple of weeks, Barbara and Laura had become really good friends. In fact, they felt as if they had known each other all their lives.

People Are More Alike Than They Are Different

No two people are exactly alike. Even so, as Laura discovered, people are more alike than they are different. All of us have a lot in common, even with our individual differences. Laura's openness and tolerance show several other points, too.

You have to keep an open mind. Find out for yourself what people are like. You might hear a lot about someone before you meet him or her. But no matter what others say, you may react to him or her differently. You may find out that the other person has many things in common with you.

Laura had heard a lot of bad things about African Americans in general. But the whispers Laura had over-heard were wrong. The people talking about the Kendalls had let their prejudice and intolerance speak for them. They had never actually met the Kendalls. But they had already decided what the family was like.

Tolerance takes courage. As Laura discovered, putting tolerance into action sometimes takes a great deal of courage. Laura did feel a little scared when she first approached Barbara. But she kept her ears, eyes, and mind open. She listened and observed for herself, and then made up her own mind. Laura did the right thing.

Her tolerance and acceptance helped Barbara feel wel-
come in her new neighborhood. It also allowed Laura
herself to find a new friend.

People should be treated as individuals. Every
individual is a little bit different from other people. One
person might be short, another tall. One individual might
be Jewish, another Baptist, and a third Muslim. One
person might be shy, another outgoing. One person
might be straight, another gay.

One trait can never tell you everything about an
individual. You may know one thing about a person or a
group of people. You may know their skin color or
religion or height or size. But that does not mean you
know everything about them.

Imagine hearing someone say, "All people with blond
hair are bubble-headed." You would immediately know
that that person was talking nonsense. Almost everyone
knows that this kind of stereotype is ridiculous. Negative
statements that begin, "All Jews...," or "All blacks...," or
"All women...," are equally untrue. These stereotypes are
not only ridiculous, but harmful.

Tolerant people never use these ugly stereotypes.
They treat people as individuals. But tolerant people look
beyond these differences. They see the things that are the
same, too. Tolerant people know that there is much more

to a person than skin color or a different language. They refuse to make judgments based on these differences.

Tolerance can catch on. If one person is willing to take the first step, tolerance can spread to others. Laura set an example when she treated Barbara with tolerance. Most of her friends quickly showed tolerance also.

Sadly, not all of Laura's friends followed her example. The world does not work so simply. Some people are afraid of anyone who seems different. Their fear keeps them intolerant and ignorant. They cling to their prejudices no matter how many times they are proved wrong. As we learned from what happened in Nazi Germany, fear and intolerance can spread to others.

Most people would rather give others the benefit of the doubt. But sometimes they need another person's heroic example. If they see an example of tolerance, a lot of people will gladly follow it. Often, all it takes is one individual reaching out and supporting someone of a different color (or sex or religion). That one person could be you or one of your friends.

Glossary: *Explaining New Words*

apartheid A political and economic system in South Africa. It allows separate, unequal, and unfair treatment of non-whites.

assumptions Guesses not necessarily based on fact.

compromise A settlement reached when each side is willing to give up some of its demands; a give and take agreement.

cooperate To work together toward a common goal.

democracy A system of government in which people hold the power, through the right to vote. In a democracy, one of the most important ideas is equal treatment for all people, regardless of race, sex, religion, or beliefs.

discrimination Negative behavior directed toward a particular group. For example, the illegal refusal to hire a person or to sell property to that person because of his or her skin color.

ignorance Being unaware; not knowing the whole truth.

injustice An action or attitude that is unfair to others or causes harm to others unfairly.

intolerance Hatred, fear, anger, or violence directed towards people simply because they differ. This difference may be race, religion, sex, appearance, ethnic or cultural background, or political beliefs.

minority group A group of people who are in some way different from most people in a group; for example, because of skin color or religious beliefs.

prejudice A negative attitude towards a group of people who share some common characteristics.

stereotype A belief that all members of a certain group act in the same manner or believe the same things.

strife Fighting or competition between two people or groups of people.

tolerance Freedom from bigotry or prejudice. Keeping an open mind towards differences of any kind. Working to unite a community in spite of differences between individuals or groups.

For Further Reading

Blume, Judy. *Iggie's House*. New York: Bradley Press, 1970.
When an African American family moves into an all-
white neighborhood, a young girl makes a friend and
learns about both prejudice and tolerance.

Brown, Gene. *Anne Frank: Child of the Holocaust*.
Woodbridge: Blackbirch Press, 1992. This biography
offers the true story of a teenager's experience during
World War II. With her own words and those of the
author, the book describes how she and her family
hid from the Nazis for two years. But they needed
the help of some tolerant friends.

Houston, Jeanne W. and James D. Houston. *Farewell to
Manzanar*. New York: Bantam, 1983. The memoirs of
a young girl growing up in a Japanese internment
camp to which her family was sent during World War II.

McKissack, Patricia. *Martin Luther King, Jr.: A Man to
Remember*. Chicago: Children's Press, 1984. This book
tells the story of the civil rights leader. King was one of
the United States' greatest champions of tolerance and
understanding. He led the fight against racial intolerance
during the 1950s and 1960s.

Seuss, Dr. *The Sneetches and Other Stories*. New York: Random
House, 1961. The title story provides a vivid picture of
intolerance and discrimination. The humorous text and
illustrations show how silly prejudices really are and how
much alike we really are.

INDEX

About the Author
Kevin Osborn, a freelance writer and editor, has written over two dozen
books for children and adults, and has coauthored several volumes in the
American Heritage *History of the United States* series. In addition, he created the characters for the young adult fiction series *Not Quite Human,*
which served as the basis for two Disney Production television movies of
the same name.

Photo Credits and Acknowledgements
Cover Photo: Stuart Rabinowitz
Pages 2, 8, 22, 26, 54, Barbara Kirk; pages 10, 13, Culver Pictures, Inc.; page 17,
Dru Nadler; 19, 20–21, 30, Charles Waldron; pages 28, 32, 37, 40, 43, 48, 52,
Wide World Photos.

Design and Production: Blackbirch Graphics, Inc.